Loudon MacQueen Douglas, F.R.S.E., F.S.A. Scot.

President of the Scottish Society, Edinburgh, in Scottish National
Dress for evening wear.

THE KILT

A MANUAL OF SCOTTISH NATIONAL DRESS

By

LOUDON MACQUEEN DOUGLAS, F.R.S.E., F.S.A. Scot.

President of the Scottish Society.

EDINBURGH:
ANDREW ELLIOT
1914

PREFACE.

THE following pages contain the substance of a lecture given before the Scottish Society of Edinburgh and may serve as an introduction to the study of Scottish National Dress. The author has received many enquiries for detailed information on the subject, and has been at some pains to examine the historical data available, from the earliest times to the present day. As a result, he has given in an appendix some hints as to how the modern Scottish National Dress should be worn. It is hoped that these notes may be of special interest to members of patriotic Societies throughout the world.

In another appendix the author has given a Bibliography which is not by any means complete, but it may be of use to those who wish to pursue the matter further. In any case, it will serve to show that the study of Scottish National Dress is one of considerable magnitude.

The Scottish Society, under whose auspices this book is published, was founded in 1911 and since then has attained considerable success. It numbers amongst its members many well known Scotsmen.

The objects of the Society are as follow :—

The cultivation of Scottish National Sentiment, the preservation of Scottish Traditions, and the encouragement of the wearing of the Scottish National Dress. In order to further the work of the Society, it is proposed that Funds be set aside to provide and maintain a Club House in Edinhurgh.

The Scottish Society is composed of Ordinary, Life and Extraordinary Members; Lady Associates and Boys under 17 years of age; and the Honorary Secretary is Mr L. Gordon Sandeman, 27 Forth Street, Edinburgh, to whom great credit is due for being the first organiser of the Society.

EDINBURGH,
January 1914.

CONTENTS.

———

		PAGE
Preface	. . . . .	3-4
List of Illustrations	. . . . .	6
Scottish National Dress.	. . . .	7
Appendices .	. . . . .	32 and 38
Appendix I.—Hints on Scottish National Dress	. . . . .	32
Appendix II.—Bibliography of Scottish National Dress	. . . .	38
Index .	. . . . .	50-51-52

LIST OF ILLUSTRATIONS.

———

Loudon MacQueen Douglas, F.R.S.E., F.S.A.
Scot. President of the Scottish Society,
Edinburgh. In Scottish National Dress
for evening wear ...   .   Frontispiece

Scottish National Dress about the year 1720,
showing an Upper and Under Officer   ... Facing page 14

Scottish National Dress of about 1720, showing
one method of using the outer kilt as a
plaid or cloak...   ...   .   ,,   15

A Highland Piper of the early part of the 18th
century   ...   .   ,,   17

Council of the Scottish Society, Edinburgh   ...   ,,   32

The late David Hepburn, Esq., for some years
President of The Caledonian Society of
London   ...   .   ,,   33

Scottish National Dress for Morning Wear   ...   ,,   36

SCOTTISH NATIONAL DRESS.

THE evolution of clothes in general is
a subject which involves an immense
amount of study and to follow the reasons
for the changes of costume which have
arisen from ancient times to the present
day, is one of the most difficult of pursuits.
This is more especially so with regard to
Scottish Dress, as the literature of the subject is so large, and the evidence so con-
flicting, that it requires infinite patience to
arrive at the elementary facts.

It is desirable that we should pursue
our studies in an orderly manner and with
this end in view, I have divided the subject up into three arbitrary periods which
seem to me to mark the various transitions
which we shall have to consider.

The first of these is from pre-historic
times until the beginning of the 18th
century, say 1720; the second period
extends from 1720 to 1745, and the third
from 1745 up to the present day.

From Pre-historic Times until 1720 :—
The earliest historical records on the subject of Scottish Dress are not very clear,

and those which depend upon tradition must be regarded with considerable scepticism. Out of the material available, however, it is possible to build up a consecutive narrative, which, if looked at either from the antiquarian or the historical point of view, possesses great interest.

Scotland in pre-historic times, and, for that matter, in historic times also, was but a poor barbarous country, and its inhabitants hailed from many lands. The earliest people to inhabit the country to any extent, seem to have been the Celts, who covered a large portion of the British Isles, and whose peculiar dress was one of the earliest forms of the national costume, but it was in Ireland more especially, that the early Celts seemed to flourish. At the present day there are strong resemblances in character and language between various branches of the Celtic race, such as the Scottish, Irish, Welsh and French.

Some of the features of the dress of the ancient Irish were—the trews or straight bracca : a long cota : the cocula or upper garment and the brogues, the notable part being that the trews were of various colours and checkered like the tartan. The cota was dyed saffron yellow, a custom which possibly was introduced from eastern countries, and this particular feature of the dress is worth noticing, as saffron yellow for centuries was the colour adopted by all the British Celts. The brogue also emerges about this time as the regular footwear, and was merely a sandal level from toe to heel. It was made out of the dried skins of beasts at first, but was afterwards made of raw half tanned leather, and fastened to the foot by means of a thong made of some kind of skin.* The Highlanders of Scotland also wore these brogues, but were not partial in ancient times to any kind of foot wear at all, and even in later historical times, after the invention of boots, many people of both sexes were in the habit of walking to church bare-footed, carrying their boots over their shoulders until they got to the church-yard : a custom whose origin may be traced back to a very remote date. The buskins which suc-ceeded the sandals and which gave rise in the Highlands to the name of "red shanks," were made from undressed deer hide, the hair being worn outwards.

"The hunted red deer's undressed hide,
Their hairy buskins well supplied."
Marmion—SIR WALTER SCOTT.

The ancient Celts did not wear the kilt at all but, in common with the Gauls and ancient Britons, wore the trews and were very fond of brilliant colours, and even so

---

* Essay on Irish Dress, by Joseph C. Walker, 1786.

far back as 390 B.C., we have it on the authority of Livy and Virgil that they appeared in flaming tartan dresses before the walls of Rome in that year.* When the Romans invaded Britain in A.D. 78, they found the ancient Aryan style of costume, of which the main part was the trews, in general use, and adopted it before finally retiring from the country. It was at a much later date that the kilt gradually emerged from a confusion of different types of dress.

During the centuries which are generally described as the Middle Ages, namely from the 5th to the 15th century, there was very little progress of any kind in Scotland and the people lived a very primitive existence. It is not until the 11th century that we find anything very remarkable to record in connection with the Scottish national life. It was in 1066 that Malcolm Canmore shifted his capital from Scone in Perthshire to Dunfermline, and that was really the beginning of what we now know as the Highland Clan system, and the establishment of that curious style of feudalism which had obtained to greater development in the Eastern countries of Europe. Subsequently there was a great addition of Saxon and Norman French

---

* "Celtic Mythology" by Alex. Macbain, M.A., Celtic Magazine, 1883.

refugees to the population of Scotland, and they were welcomed by Malcolm Canmore who granted them lands and many privileges of a feudal character, and it is curious in this connection to note that the Gordons first set foot in Scotland in connection with this immigration.

As the clan system has so much to do with the development of the Scottish National Dress, it may be well to say in a few words what it really was. The clan consisted of a chief, who was the absolute law giver and leader in war. The kinsmen of the chief came next in precedence, and after them the petty chieftains who owed allegiance to the chief. Each clan had a specific rendezvous or meeting place, and all the members of the clan at a given signal were bound to repair to this place on a summons from the chief, this usually being delivered by the sending round of a fiery-cross which was delivered from hand to hand. In this way the members of the clan were gathered together in a very short time, the objects of such gatherings being, as a rule, some war-like expedition against a neighbouring clan or tribe. Obviously, to small tribes such as grew out of the Scottish feudal system, it would be desirable to have distinguishing marks, and it is possible that this is the origin of the many distinct patterns of tartan which have come into existence. The clan system which, as we have seen, arose in the 11th century, developed into a distinct national feature during the succeeding five centuries and may be said to have been crippled after 1715, and finally crushed out after 1745. It must be remembered, however, that authentic history previous to 1715, is lacking.

The principal occupation of the clans seems to have been fighting, and the development of industry of any sort did not seem to enter much into their mode of existence. The weaving of cloth by hand looms was happily one of the industries which flourished alongside of the extremely primitive agriculture. The principal colours used for cloth, were white and black, these being derived from the undyed wool and used for general purposes such as blankets, plaids, or the making of bracca or trews. As a matter of fact, however, the poverty of the country was so great that expensive dresses of any kind could not be worn, and even the chiefs, who lived in the most primitive way, were not habited very much better than the other members of the clans. One writer who has put on record his impressions of a journey through the Highlands of Scotland at a later date than that of which we speak, says :— *

* " Letters from a Gentleman in the North of Scotland to His Friend in London."

"Their cottages are in general miserable habitations ; they are built of round stones without any cement, thatched with sods, and sometimes heath ; they are generally, though not always, divided by a wicker partition into two apartments, in the larger of which the family reside : it serves likewise as a sleeping-room for them all.   In the middle of this room is the fire, made of peat placed on the floor, and over it, by means of a hook, hangs the pot for dressing the victuals.   There is frequently a hole in the roof to allow exit to the smoke ; but this is not directly over the fire, on account of the rain ; and very little of the smoke finds its way out of it, the greatest part, after having filled every corner of the room, coming out of the door, so that it is almost impossible for any one unaccustomed to it to breathe in the hut.   The other apartment, to which you enter by the same door, is reserved for cattle and poultry, when these do not choose to mess and lodge with the family." *

Under these circumstances it would be impossible to look for any refinements in dress, and the simplest method of clothing the body would undoubtedly be the one which appealed to the vast majority of the people.   It is very easy to understand how

---

* Garnett's Tour, quoted by Capt. Burt in His Letters.

the saffron shirt and the belted plaid came into general use.   Both are similar in character to the Celtic costume which was common in Ireland and Wales, and it was not until well on in the 17th century that any marked improvements took place. The original Highland plaid or breacan-feile, which literally means a variegated or checkered covering, consisted of a plain piece of tartan from 4 to 6 yards in length and 2 yards broad, it was "folded or pleated round the waist and firmly bound with a leather belt so that the lower side fell down to below the knee joint and, while there were the foldings behind, the cloth was double in front. The upper part was then fastened to the shoulder with a large brooch or pin, the two ends being sometimes suffered to hang down on the right side or more usually tucked under the belt."*

Another description is given by Rogers, who says:—

"We are indebted for the following description to Colonel Ross of Cromarty. 'Their ancient dress was the breacan feile or kilted plaid. This consisted of from 7 to 12 yards of tartan sewn up the middle so as to form a plaid of double width varying from 4 to 6 yards long, by 2 yards in

---

* "The Ancient Highlander," by John S. Keltie, F.S.A. Scot.

Scottish National Dress about the year 1720.

Showing an Upper and Under Officer.

Scottish National Dress of about 1720.

Showing one method of using the Outer Kilt as a Plaid or Cloak.

width. Highland looms did not fabricate tartan wider than one yard. A portion of this length was laid on the ground with the belt under it; the lower and middle portion being then plaited so as to form a kilt, leaving a flap at each side. The Highlander now lay down upon it, crossed the right flap, and next placed the left flap over it, and buckled his belt. When he got up, the upper part of the plaid, which formed a sort of double kilt, was fastened with a piece of deer's horn or a brooch on his left shoulder, and part of the plaid on the right side was tucked under the belt. To the waist-belt was attached the sporran, usually made of leather with a brass or silver mouthpiece, so constructed that persons unacqainted with the secret could not open it. The ancient sporran did not hang loose, but the waist-belt was passed through two rings on the mouthpiece which made it fast to the person. A dirk and one or two pistols were also worn on the waist-belt. By undoing the waist-belt the plaid was made to form a blanket, in which the Highlander could at night envelop himself." *

Capt. Burt also says that "when the Highlanders are trained to lie amongst the hills in cold, dry, windy weather, they sometimes soak the plaid in some river or

* "Social Life in Scotland," by Charles Rogers.

burn, and then holding the corner up above their heads, they turn themselves round and round until they are enveloped in the whole mantle, and then lay themselves down on the leeward side of some hill where the wet and warmth of their bodies make a steam like that of a boiling kettle, and keep them warm by thickening the stuff and keeping the wind from penetrating."

It was not till early in the 18th century that the kilt emerged as a separate part of the costume. The tartan itself is described in Capt. Burt's Letters from the Highlands as—

" The chequered stuff, commonly worn by the Highlanders, by them called *breacan* (parti-coloured), and by the Lowlanders *tartan* (Fr. tiretaine), is neither peculiar to Celts nor Goths, and is to be found, at this day, although not in such general use, among many of the Sclavonic tribes, who have no connection with either.

That the Lowlanders had their tartan from the French, at a time when it was fashionable in other countries, may be presumed from the name ; and to imagine that the manufacture began among the Highlanders would be ridiculous."[*]

It may be taken that as Capt. Burt wrote in 1730, he was well in touch with

[*] " Letters from a gentleman in the North of Scotland to his friend in London."

A Highland Piper of the early part of the 18th Century.

the facts and his valuable book is regarded as one of the most authentic in connection with the history of the Scottish Highlands.

Pinkerton, whose general collection of voyages and travels published in 1808 are well known, states that the kilt is not ancient, but is singular and adapted to the savage life of the Highlanders.

It is a curious thing to note in this connection that few of the paintings of Highland Chiefs or Scottish Noblemen, which belong to the early part of the 17th century, are shown with either tartan or the kilted costume, although there is no doubt of both being worn then. The sculptured stones of Scotland such as those found at Dupplin in Perthshire ; Forres in Moray-shire; and Nigg in Ross-shire, show figures with some kind of resemblance to the kilted Scottish Dress. The armorial bearings of the Burnets of Leys (1626), and the Mackenzies of Coull (1693) show what appears to be the modern kilt, but there is no evidence whatever to show that this form of wearing the kilt, as separated from the belted plaid, was in general use. Unhappily, in those days, there were no journals to record the doings of the times, as the first newspaper to be published in Scotland, and entitled "The Mercurious Scotticus" appeared only on the 5th August 1651.

We have already seen that for a long

c

period the belted plaid was the principal item of Scottish Dress. It was then succeeded by the little kilt, which was made of six ells of single tartan being pleated and sewn, and which was fixed round the waist with a strap, half-a-yard being left plain at each end, and these crossed each other in front. The little kilt was called the feile beg or fillibeg, and was much the same in appearance as the kilt worn at the present day, the origin of which, however, must be referred to a much later date than that of the little kilt.

In considering these early dresses, it must be borne in mind that the weapons carried by the Highlander formed an essential part of his costume, and the reason for the belted plaid being fastened over the left shoulder was obviously that the right arm might be free. Perhaps as good a description as any of the equipment of the Highlander in the 17th century is that given by Mr M'Intyre North,* who says :

"Now to complete this grand dress, they wear a broad sword, which they call a claymore, a stroke of which delivered from one of their hands, would be sufficient to chop off the head of the strongest champion that ever lived; they wear a pair of pistols, and a dirk, which resembles a

---

* "The Book of the Club of True Highlanders," by C. N. M'Intyre North.

dagger, intended chiefly for stabbing—this
weapon hangs before in a scabbard, along
with a knife and fork, and purse for their
money, which they term a sporran; next,
they have a large powder horn that they
hang across their shoulders, with a small
belt studded with brass nails; and to finish
the dress, they wear a target, composed
of leather, wood or brass, and which is so
strong, that no ball can penetrate it, and in
the middle of the target there is a screw
hole, wherein is fixed a brass cup, lined
with horn, and which serves them to drink
out of upon occasions, and in the time of
action it serves to fix a bayonet in.   Thus
accoutred they make a most splendid and
glorious appearance, it being esteemed by
all judges to be the most heroic and majes-
tic habit ever worn by any nation; but at
present they are prohibited the use of their
ancient clothing.   A broadsword, target,
pistols, dirk and powder horn are part of
their paternal heritage and without these
weapons they seldom or never go abroad."

It was the habit of the Highlanders when
going into battle to discharge their firearms
at the enemy and immediately thereafter to
proceed to divest themselves of the plaid
and their upper clothing, rushing at their
foes claymore in hand, the body being
partially covered by their targes.   This
particular mode of fighting was responsible

in early Scottish history, for gaining many victories over trained troops, but, as we shall see, proved fatal at the last stand the Highlanders ever made in Scotland. On the march they had, in addition to their other equipment, a side pouch or darloch in which they carried provisions, and these were of an extremely simple character, the general rule being a supply of coarse oatmeal which was either soaked in a little water or licked dry out of the hand. Generally speaking, the conditions to which we have referred prevailed prior to the Rebellion of 1715. After that date we are in a position to record much more authentically the developments of Scottish National Dress, and this brings us to what we may describe as the second period in its transition.

From 1720 to 1745.

The Rebellion of 1715 was a badly conducted affair, and James Stuart, the Pretender to the throne, was soon driven overseas before the victorious forces of George the First, but the latter, who had a distinct animus against everything that was Scottish, proceeded to enact oppressive laws against all who had taken part in the rising. As a consequence, the carrying of arms and the wearing of the Scottish dress in the Highland districts were prohibited, but although these enactments continued for a time, it soon became apparent that the goodwill of the Scottish people to the Hanoverian Succession would never be gained by such means. The oppressive measures, therefore, were gradually withdrawn, and the Scottish dress became more and more a distinct national feature. It was about this time that the word *kilt* came into general use, and it seems to have been of Lowland origin. It is a Lowland word signifying a shortened or tucked-up garment. The use of the word *fillibeg* was then, to a large extent, discontinued. The plaid also figured largely at this time in Lowland politics, and it will be remembered that Allan Ramsay, who was strongly Jacobite, and who opposed the Union in 1707, wrote a poem entitled "Tartana, or the Plaid," which specially refers to the wearing of tartan plaids by the ladies, a custom which at that time was universal all over the Lowlands, and he, in common with many others of the time, strongly insisted on the national character of the tartans :— *

"Oh, first of garbs, garments of happy fate :
    So long employed, of such an antique date ;
Look back to some thousand years till records fail,
    And loose themselves in some romantic tale ;
We'll find our god-like fathers nobly scorned
    To be by any other dress adorned."

ALLAN RAMSAY.

---

* "The Highland Dress" by J. G. Mackay.

It may be well to refer here to the minor parts of the Scottish Dress and to say that a completely equipped Highland Chief about this time would have the following :—*

No. 1.   A full-trimmed bonnet.
No. 2.   A tartan jacket, vest, kilt and cross-belt.
No. 3.   A tartan belted plaid.
No. 4.   Pair of hose made up (of cloth).
No. 5.   Pair of stockings, ditto, with yellow garters.
No. 6.   Two pairs of brogues.
No. 7.   A silver-mounted purse and belt.
No. 8.   A target with spear.
No. 9.   A broad-sword.
No. 10. A pair of pistols and bullet mould.
No. 11. A dirk, knife, fork, and belt.

The bonnet was always a distinct feature and was mostly always blue with a red checkered rim and sometimes a red tassel, there being many varied shapes.

The ancient form of stocking varied considerably from the soleless osan to the tartan stockings cut out of the web of the cloth, but these have been supplanted by knitted fabrics and the ancient brogues have given place to the modern boot or shoe. The gaiter is a feature, the origin of which is of interest. White gaiters are worn by the Highland

---

* "The Clans, Septs and Regiments of the Scottish Highlands," by Frank Adam, F.R.G.S., F.S.A. Scot.

Regiments in memory of some of the trials which they underwent in the Peninsular War. It was during the retreat of the forces under Sir John Moore at Corunna that the soldiers suffered great hardships, their boots becoming worn owing to the rocky nature of the ground on the Portuguese coast. The Highlanders took the shirts from their backs, tore them into stripes and bound them round their feet for protection, and this did not fail to attract considerable notice at home, as the white spats or gaiters were instituted in memory of these trying times. In modern times, many modifications have crept in such as: the addition of silver shoe buckles to the shoes and highly ornamental sporrans, mostly made from goats' hair. The original sporrans were made from the skins of wild animals, such as the badger or the otter, but several historical personages have also worn these of velvet or other strong cloth. Garters were made in rich colours and very broad, but that custom has fallen away, for the garter is now generally concealed by a fold in the stocking. The skean-dhu or small dirk is generally fixed under the garter of the right leg. During the 18th century the wealthy were generally clothed with the short coat and waist coat adorned with solid silver buttons, tassels, embroidery or lace; all of which was regulated by individual taste and, as a consequence, a great variety of designs may be seen in such portraits as have been handed down to us. These designs are so various, that it is quite impossible to lay down any general rule which would apply to all. Indeed, the only portion of the dress which does not vary is the kilt itself.

There was a reason in earlier times for the use of silver buttons, as it was thought that, should their wearer fall in battle, the value of the buttons would provide him with a decent funeral. This idea was carried to such an extent, that in the 17th century it is said that the officers of Mackay's and Munroe's regiment, which went to Sweden to serve under Gustavus Adolphus, had rich buttons on their clothes and that they also wore each a solid chain round the neck, so as to ensure the owner, if wounded or taken prisoner, good treatment.*

The laws proscribing the wearing of the kilt or the carrying of arms continued to be enforced in the Highlands for a good many years after the Rebellion of 1715, but they were practically a dead letter in the South of Scotland, and it is largely owing to this fact that tartan was preserved as a feature of the national dress. The greatest impetus, however, was given to the wearing

---

* "History of the Highlanders—Highland Clans," by James Browne, LL.B.

of the costume by the formation of the Highland Companies which were employed in the disarming of the Highlanders, preventing depredation, bringing criminals to justice and hindering rebels and attainted persons from inhabiting the northern part of the kingdom.*

When General Wade in 1725 was sent to Scotland to pacify the Highlands, in pursuance of the act for disarming the Highlanders, he gave orders that the six companies in existence should adopt a uniform tartan, and this being of a dark colour, gave rise to the name of the Black Watch, of which these six companies were the nucleus. It was not however, till 1739 that the companies were formed into a regiment and their glorious history began. There can be little doubt however, that the intention of raising the Black Watch was that the regiment should be kept in Scotland, and that the Government sent them to England by a series of false statements. Subsequently, the intentions of the Government were made plain, as in 1743 the regiment was sent to Flanders and gave a splendid account of itself at Fontenoy. The tartan of the Black Watch is entirely of an arbitrary description, and has no clan significance at all, but it has always

---

* General Wade's Report.

D

been associated with some of the greatest
deeds accomplished by the British army.
The mutiny in the Black Watch which
took place on the real intentions of the
Government being disclosed, has been fully
told by Mr MacWilliam* and the subsequent execution of mutineers which took
place in the Tower of London, is one of
the darkest pages in the history of the regiment.   The great success of the Black
Watch caused other Highland Regiments
to be formed, such as the 71st in 1773;
the 72nd in the same year; the 74th in
1788; the 78th in 1793; the 79th or
Cameron Highlanders in 1795; the 92nd
or Gordon Highlanders in 1796; and the
93rd or Sutherland Highlanders in 1800.
The Black Watch has been linked up with
the Gordon Highlanders: the 71st and
74th are now the Highland Light Infantry;
the 72nd and 78th are known as the Sea-
forth Highlanders; the 75th and 92nd, the
Gordon Highlanders; the 91st and 93rd,
the Argyle and Sutherland Highlanders,
whereas, the 79th remains still the Queen's
Own Cameron Highlanders.   At the present day however, the nationality of the
members of these regiments is not exclus-
ively Scottish, there being about 75 per
cent. Scottish or of Scottish descent, the

---

* "The Black Watch Mutiny Records" H. D. MacWilliam.

remainder being English, Welsh and Irish.

The dress of these regiments has become quite a national feature and has done more than anything else to perpetuate the wearing of the kilt. It would take too long to describe the differences which characterise each regiment, suffice it to say that there are modifications of the ancient costume of sufficiently marked character to make the dress of each regiment distinct by itself.

We have already referred to the war with France and to the exploits of the Black Watch at Fontenoy. The troubles of England with her continental neighbours were not lost upon the Jacobites, who still had hopes of restoring the Stuart dynasty, and in 1744 the French Government placed Charles Edward Stuart, the grandson of James II., at the head of a formidable army with the intention of descending upon Scotland, but the plan was frustrated by a storm and the invasion never took place. Undaunted, however, the young Pretender started out in 1745 with seven friends in a small vessel for the shores of Scotland, hoping in this way to arouse the Jacobite spirit. It was on the 29th August that the clans rallied to his standard in Glenfinnan, and he proceeded to Edinburgh with an army which continually increased as he went along. In Edinburgh he was proclaimed James VIII. at the Town Cross

On 21st September, General Sir John
Cope, who had been sent against him with
2000 English troops, was routed, and had
to flee before the victorious clansmen at
Prestonpans, and the success of this engage-
ment increased the troops under Prince
Charles's command up to about 6000. An
army was collected at Newcastle to oppose
his march South, but he decided to go by
Lancashire, and on the 4th December
got as far as Derby. Here his good for-
tune left him, and the subsequent events
made up one long tragedy, not only to
himself but to his followers. The Jacobites
of Lancashire who had promised so much,
turned aloof, and only one single squire in
that county came to his assistance. The
Jacobite army of now, about 4000 men, had
nothing left but to retreat and fell back on
Glasgow, where accessions to the army
brought up the number to about 9000, and
the battle of Falkirk on the 23rd January
1746, immediately followed. The victory
was certainly with Prince Charles, but by
the irony of fate, several thousand of his
Highlanders having secured plenty of
booty, scattered and returned to their
native hills. Retreat was the only thing
left, and with some 6000 men the Prince
found himself on Culloden Moor on the
16th April, 1746, faced by the skilled
troops of the Duke of Cumberland in

command of a force of nearly 12,000 men.
The gallant Highlanders tried their old
tactics of flinging themselves on the front
of the enemy, but the musketry of the
trained soldiers swept them down in
hundreds, and the few who burst through
the first line of the royal troops did so only
to find themselves face to face with another
unbroken line in the rear. The battle of
Culloden was all over in a short time and
the Prince was a fugitive. After romantic
adventures and hair-breadth escapes, he
escaped to France, and the last hope of the
Stuarts had gone. It was the last organised
attempt also of the Scottish clans to act
together, and with the Battle of Culloden
the clan system came to end.

These brief references to this romantic
epoch in history are necessary so as to
understand the subsequent fortunes of the
Scottish National Dress. In 1746 the wearing of the tartan was prohibited by law and a
series of oppressive measures were at once
introduced providing heavy penalties for
all who either carried arms or wore the
kilt, and it was not till 1782 that these
harsh measures were repealed. In the
thirty-six intervening years, the weaving of
tartan had entirely ceased in the Highlands, and to such an extent had the repressive laws been effective, that many of the
old settes were entirely forgotten and, but

for the fact that in the Lowlands, particularly in Edinburgh, tartan was worn in
spite of the repressive laws, it is possible
that the making of the ancient fabrics would
have become merely a memory.   It was
due very largely to the ladies of the capital
city that the tartan became quite a fashionable craze, and, to such an extent that
plaids and gowns of tartan were considered
the only correct things to wear.   One
authority states that even the bed and
window curtains and the pin cushions of
the ladies were all made of tartan.*

From 1746 *to the present day :—*

The third period in the history of Scottish
Dress may be said to have begun in 1746.
During the following thirty-six years a
policy of extinction was carried out, but it
was defeated by the popularity of the tartan
in the Lowlands, so that from 1782 onwards
the wearing of the tartan became general
all over Scotland.   There arose also at that
time the great Wizard of the North, and he
peopled the country with romantic figures
which did much to revive the popularity of
the Highlands of Scotland, and gave quite
a new interest to the wearing of the National
Dress.   From then until now, there is little
to chronicle in connection with the Scottish
National Dress, except that it has become

---

* "A Short History of the Scottish Highlands," by W. C.
MacKenzie.

the emblem of Scotsmen in whatever part of the world they happen to be placed. The patriotic Scottish Societies throughout the world have done much to encourage the wearing of the kilt, and at the present day there is a strong feeling throughout the Scottish race that the national costume with the romantic history attached to it, should always be worn by every patriot who is proud of the traditions of his country.

APPENDIX.—I.

HINTS ON SCOTTISH NATIONAL DRESS.

The following are some notes on Scottish National Dress which indicate the manner in which it should be worn at the present day.

The modern Scottish National Dress is a modification of the ancient costume which has passed through many variations before reaching the present form.

The salient features of the present day *Evening Dress* are as follows :—

The Kilt.

The kilt should be worn so that when the wearer is standing erect, the edge of it should reach the centre of the knee-cap. The kilt is, of course, the principal part of the Scottish dress, and should be made of tartan associated with the name of the wearer. In the absence of any claim to wear a particular tartan, the Royal Stuart tartan can be worn.

The Doublet.

There is considerable variety in the form of the doublet, but when this is made of ordinary broadcloth, it should have lapels, and gauntlets on the sleeves, silver or silver-mounted buttons of the diamond shape being used throughout. The buttons may either have a thistle or the Scottish Lion inscribed upon them, or any other legend, according to the resources of the wearer.

The Vest.

The vest should be of the same coloured cloth as the doublet, and should have lapels over the lower

Council of the Scottish Society, Edinburgh.

W. Strachan.   Dr Pirie Watson.   Major A. M'Donald.   George Fraser Dobie.

L. Gordon Sandeman,   W. H. Cameron Kirkland,   Loudon MacQueen Douglas,   W. Sutherland M'Kay,

Hon. Secretary.   M.A., Ll.B.,   F.R.S.E., F.S.A. Scot.,   *Hon. Treasurer.*

Vice President   *President.*

The late David Hepburn, Esq.
For some years President of The Caledonian Society of London.

The Scottish National Dress, showing the manner of wearing Ruffles
with a Velvet Doublet.

pockets. Coloured vests are quite in order, but it should be borne in mind that the scarlet vest is more worn by men-servants than by others, and as a rule should be discarded in ordinary evening dress.

The Coatee.

In place of the doublet some Scottish dresses have a coatee, or short coat, with abbreviated tails, like a morning coat. It is quite optional whether this is worn, or the doublet. Any form of the Coatee, however, is entirely modern, and, personally, I prefer the doublet. I understand that in some parts of the North of Scotland they are trying to introduce a coatee with longer coat tails, and if this succeeds I think it will be a pity, as the doublet strikes me as being much more complete and artistic than any form of the coatee that I have seen. It is, however, a matter for one's own personal taste.

The Plaid.

The plaid is merely ornamental, but should always be worn with evening dress. The lower end of the plaid is fastened round the waist by a band, and the other end is pulled through the epaulette on the left shoulder. At this point there should be a rosette on the plaid through which, after it has been drawn through the epaulette, a brooch is fixed. This brooch may be of almost any design, provided it is circular, and may have a stone (Cairngorm or other) in the centre, or be after the pattern of the Lorne brooch. A circular ring of chased silver looks as well as anything else, and is quite in keeping with tradition. The brooch should always be fastened just on the edge of the epaulette on the left shoulder.

Tie, etc.

The adopted form of scarf is the lace jabot, and the modern combination is with the jabot and the ordinary

E

starched collar. To those who prefer it, however, there is no reason why soft stock collars should not be worn, but they are not always so becoming as the starched collar. With gauntlets on the sleeves it is not necessary to wear lace ruffles. These, as a matter of fact, are quite optional, and are comparatively modern, being introduced about the 18th century. So far as I can make out, they have been generally worn with velvet doublets, but in that case the doublets would not have gauntlets.

The shirt to be worn with the evening dress should, preferably, have a soft front, and the pleated variety seems to me to be the most comfortable.

Trews.

Short trews should always be worn with evening dress.

Stockings and Foot Wear.

Stockings used to be made out of the web of tartan, but are now knitted, and can be obtained in any pattern. The most convenient stockings are those which come right up to under the knee-cap, with a fold on the top which should turn down over garters, to which are attached tartan ribbons of the same tartan as the stockings. These two projecting ribbons should appear below the fold of the stockings on the outside of the limbs.

Boots should never be worn with evening dress: brogues, preferably with silver buckles, are the most convenient.

Cap.

The best form of cap to accompany evening dress is of the flat, circular Balmoral shape.

Ornaments.

The shoulder brooch has already been referred to but, in addition to this, there should be a dirk, com posed of a single-edged sheath knife, and knife and fork, all in one sheath, and which should be suspended from a broad belt with a triangular-shaped piece of leather to keep it in position. The belt is fastened round the waist under the vest, and the dirk should hang just in front of the first lapel of the doublet on the right side, so that it can be seen from the front. It is very necessary to have a triangular-shaped piece of leather from which to suspend the dirk, as otherwise it is impossible to keep it in position.

The Skean dhu is a small dagger which should be placed under the garter of the right leg, being worn to the outside.

The sporran for evening dress should be of goat's hair with tassels, and the lower fringe should fall below the edge of the kilt, about an inch. There are many different kinds of sporrans, some of these being small, and others highly ornamented. The goat's hair sporran, however, is most generally used, and is very becoming. Small circular sporrans are more suitable for morning wear than otherwise.

Other ornaments may consist of a claw brooch to fasten the edges of the kilt, but this is highly objectionable for dancing, as the claw is apt to catch the dresses of the ladies. The simplest fastener for the kilt is a large silver safety pin. Sometimes other ornaments are worn, such as a brooch in the jabot, a broad belt round the waist, which was at one time used for the carrying of pistols, and also supported the belted plaid and sporran. These belts have large rectangular silver buckles, but are seldom worn at the present day.

Similar broad belts which also have large rectangular silver buckles in front, are occasionally worn over the shoulder. These belts were meant for carrying the claymore, which, obviously, is not a portion of evening dress.

I have also seen powder horns carried over the shoulder, but I think that such a decoration is incongruous.

The evening dress as indicated in these notes is

meant to be such a dress as can be comfortably worn, and it is certainly not desirable to overload the body with weighty ornaments. In its simplicity the Scottish National Dress is not only handsome, but it is the most comfortable of all costumes.

Morning Dress.

Morning dress is a very simple affair and consists of Balmoral cap, tweed jacket and vest, with plain horn buttons. The jacket and vest should be made of the lapel pattern with plain epaulettes on the shoulders. The kilt should be made of heavier material than that worn for evening dress, but that is a matter of choice. The sporran should be either of plain leather, or badger, but in any case should be of the small round pattern. Stockings should be of ordinary hose material, and should not be of tartan.

Foot wear should consist of thick soled brogues with gaiters to match the stockings. Where gaiters are not worn the tongue of the brogue should project over the instep about two inches. The only weapon worn with morning dress is the Skean dhu in the right leg. Collar and tie should be of the ordinary pattern, the bow tie being most becoming for this style of dress.

LADIES' DRESS.

It is desirable that ladies who wish to encourage the Scottish National Dress should wear sashes of tartan, with evening dress. These should be preferably worn over the left shoulder and fixed by a circular brooch. Other applications of the tartan in connection with ladies' costume must be left very largely to personal taste.

Scottish National Dress for Morning Wear.

SCOTTISH NATIONAL DRESS FOR LEVEES.

The following are the directions issued by the Lord Chamberlain's Office, St James's Palace, London, for Scottish National Dress for Levees.

Black silk velvet full dress doubtlet. Silk lined.

Set of silver celtic or crest buttons for doublet.

Superfine tartan full dress kilt.

Short trews.

Full dress tartan stockings.

Full dress long shoulder plaid.

Full dress white hair sporran. Silver-mounted and tassels.

Patent leather and silver chain strap for sporran.

Full dress silver-mounted dirk with knife and fork.

Full dress silver-mounted skean dhu.

Patent leather shoulder belt, silver-mounted.

Patent leather waist belt, silver clasp.

Silver-mounted shoulder brooch.

Silver kilt pin.

Lace jabot.

One pair of buckles for instep of shoes.

One pair small ankle buckles for shoes.

Full dress brogues.

Highland claymore.

Glengarry or Balmoral, crest or ornament.

APPENDIX.—II.

BIBLIOGRAPHY
OF SCOTTISH DRESS.

Dialogue between Eudoxus and Irenoeus, by Edmund Spenser; from The Ancient History of Ireland, containing Spenser's view of the state of Ireland, 1596. Dublin, printed by the Society of Stationers, 1633. Reprinted at the Hibernia Press, Temple Lane, by John Morrison, 1809.

Celtic Mythology by Alexander Macbain, M.A., The Celtic Magazine, 1883.

Essay on Irish Dress by Joseph C. Walker, from the Milesian Invasion to the end of the Stewart Period. Printed for T. Payne & Son at the News Gate, London, 1786.

Historical Essay on the Dress of the Ancient and Modern Irish, Joseph C. Walker, Dublin. Geo. Grierson, 1788.

British Costume, Mrs Chas. H. Ashdown, London, T. C. & E. C. Jack, 16 Henrietta Street, and Edinburgh, 1910.

Antiquities of Ireland, by Edward Ledwich, LL.B., M.R.I.A. & F.S.A., London and Scotland. Dublin, printed for Arthur Grueber, 59 Dame Street, 1790.

Memoirs of Scottish Affairs from 1624 to 1651.

The Costume of the Ancients by Thomas Hope. Printed by W. Balmer & Co., Cleveland Row, St James', London, 1809.

Early Travellers in Scotland, edited by P. Hume Brown. Edinburgh, David Douglas, 1891.

History of the Province of Moray, by Lachlan Shaw. Enlarged and brought down to the present time by J. F. S. Gordon. Glasgow, printed at the University Press and published by Hamilton Adams & Co., London. Thos. D. Morison, Glasgow, 1882.

A Social History of Ireland, by P. W. Joyce. Longmans Green & Co., 39 Paternoster Row, 1903.

Womenkind in all Ages of Western Europe, by Thos. Wright, M.A., F.S.A., Hon. M.R.S.L. London, Groombridge & Sons, Paternoster Row, 1849.

On the Manners and Customs of the Ancient Irish, by Eugene O'Curry, M.R.I.A., with Introduction by W. K. Sullivan, Ph.D. Williams & Norgate, 14 Henrietta Street, Covent Garden, London, 1873, and 20 S. Frederick Street, Edinburgh.

James Robertson's Tour through some of the Western Islands and West Coast of Scotland in 1768: a paper communicated to the Society of Antiquaries of Scotland by Sir James Foulis of Colinton, 1788 Inserted in the Proceedings of the Society of Antiquaries of Scotland, 1897.

The Ancient Costume of the Irish, by T.P.M. The Celt, 1858. Dublin, John O'Daly, 9 Anglesea St.

The Descriptive Catalogue in the Museum of the R.I. Academy, by W. R. Wilde. Dublin, 1863, R.I.A. House, Dawson Street.

The Encyclopædia Britannica.

Scandinavia, by Andrew Crichton, LL.D., and Henry Wheaton, LL.D. Edinburgh, Oliver & Boyd, Tweeddale Court, 1838.

The Complete Irish Traveller. Printed for the Proprietors and sold by the Booksellers, 1788.

Ireland, under Elizabeth and James I., described by Edmund Spenser, edited by Henry Morley, LL.D. Geo. Routledge & Sons, Ltd., Broadway, Ludgate Hill, 1890.

The Manners and Customs of the Ancient Irish, by Eugene O'Curry, M.R.I.A., with introduction by W. K. Sullivan, Ph.D., 1873.

The Church and Shrine of St. Manchan, by the Rev. James Graves, A.B., M.R.I.A. Journal of the Royal Historical and Arch. Association of Ireland, 1874-5. Dublin, printed at the University Press, 1876.

Proceedings of the Antiquaries of Scotland, Edinburgh. Printed for the Society by Neill & Co.

Notes on a pair of Pampooties or shoes of raw hide from Aran More, Galway Bay, by A. J. G. Mackay, LL.D.,

F.S.A., and On Cuaran and other varieties of shoes used in the Highlands and Islands of Scotland, by Alex. Carmichael. Proceedings of the Society of Antiquaries, 1894.

The Shamrock in Literature, by Nathaniel Colgan, M.R.I.A., R.S. of Antiq. of Ireland, 1896.

Antiquity explained and represented in sculpture by the Learned Father Montfaucon. Translated into English by David Humphrets, M.A. London, printed by J. Tonson and J. Watts, 1721.

Three Years' Travels over England, Scotland and Wales, by James Broome, M.A. London, printed for Rob. Gosling at the Mitre, over against Chancery Lane, 1707.

A Tour in England and Scotland by an Englishman (Mr Thomas Newte). London, 1788, printed for G. G. J. and J. Robinson, Paternoster Row.

History of Edinburgh, by Hugo Arnot. Printed for Mr Wm. Greech, 1787.

Historical Memoirs of the Irish Bards, by Joseph Walker. Printed 1786. London, printed for T. Payne at the New's Gate, and G. G. J. and J. Robinson, Paternoster Row.

Britannia, by W. Gamden, enlarged by latest discoveries by R. Gough. London, printed for John Stockdale, Piccadilly, by S. Godnell, Little Queen Street, 1806.

The Gentleman's Magazine, 1750, Article by Sylvanus Urban. London, printed by Edward Cave, 1750.

Drawings and Dissertation respecting some Roman Antiquities discovered on the Line of Antonine's Vallum since the publication of General Roy's work, by Rev. J. Skinner, A.M., F.S.A., Archæologia, 1827.

The Image of Irelande with a Discourie of Woodkarne, by John Derricke, 1581. Edinburgh, Adam and Chas. Black, 1883.

Concise Historical Proofs respecting the Gael of Alban, or Highlanders of Scotland, by James A. Robertson, F.S.A., Scotland. Edinburgh, Wm. P. Nimmo: London, Marshall & Co., 1867.

A New History of Scotland from the earliest accounts of its population down to the Year of Our Lord, 1783. Edinburgh, John Brown, 1783. (Some points of resemblance between the Gauls and the Gaels).

The World's Inhabitants by G. T. Bettany, M.A. Ward Lock & Co., London, Warwick House, Salisbury Square, E.C., 1888.

Tytler's History of Scotland, London, Glasgow and Edinburgh.

The Ancient Highlanders, by John S. Keltie, F.S.A. Scot. A. Fullarton & Co., Edinburgh, 1875.

The Highlanders of Scotland, by W. S. Skene, LL.D., F.S.A. Scot. Aeneas Mackay, 43 Murray Place, Stirling, 1902.

M'Ian's Highlanders at Home, or Gaelic Gatherings. London, Ackermann & Co., Strand, 1848.

Clans of Highlanders of Scotland, being an account of their annals separately and collectively, with delineations of their Tartans, and family Arms, edited by Thomas Smibert. Edinburgh, James Hogg. Glasgow, D. Robertson. London, R. Groombridge & Sons, 1850.

Journey through the West Part of the Scotch Highlands, by Robert Heron. Perth, R. Morrison, jun. 1793.

The Highland Garb, by J. Mackay. Transactions of the Gaelic Society of Inverness, 1878.

A Short Account of Scotland, by Thomas Morer, Minister of St Ann's without Aldersgate, when he was Chaplain to a Scotch Regiment. London, printed for John Morphew, near Stationer's Hall, 1715.

A New Description of Orkney, Zetland, etc., 1700, by John Brand Edinburgh, printed by G. M., 1703.

An Account of the Isle of Man with a voyage to Isle of Columb-Kill, by William Sacheverell, Late Governor of the Man. London, printed for J. Hartley, 1702.

A Classical Tour through Italy, by the Rev. J. Chetwode Eustace. London, printed for J. Mawman, 39 Ludgate Street, 1815.

Full and Particular Description of the Highlands of Scotland, by John Campbell. London, printed for the author, 1752.

The Present State of the Orkney Islands, by James Fea, Surgeon, Holyrood House, 1775.

Travels in the Western Hebrides, 1782-90, by the Rev. John Lane Buchanan, A.M. London, printed for G. G. J. and J. Robinson, Paternoster Row.

The History of Domestic Manners and Sentiments in England during the Middle Ages, by Thos. Wright, M.A., F.S.A. London, Chapman & Hall, 193 Piccadilly, 1862.

Musical Instruments and their Homes, by Mary E. and Wm. A. Brown, New York, 1888. Dodd, Mead & Co.

Musical Memoirs, by John G. Dalyell. Thos. G. Stevenson, Edinburgh, 1849.

The Highland Bagpipe, from the Celtic Magazine, 1884.

The Supplement to Antiquity explained and represented in sculpture, by the learned Father Montfaucon. Translated into English by David Humphrets, M.A. London, printed by J. Tonson and J. Watts, 1725.

The Bagpipe, Britannica Encyclopaedia, 1910. Cambridge University Press.

The Highland Bagpipe, by W. L. Manson (including notes on the Highland Garb). Alexander Gardner, Paisley and London, 26 Paternoster Square, 1901.

Feud of the Clans, by Alex. MacGregor, M.A., Stirling, 1907.

History of Scotland, by Malcolm Laing, 1804.

War Cries of Irish Septs., Ulster Journal of Archæology, 1855.

The Present State of Great Britain, by John Chamberlayne. London, 1708.

History of Scots Affairs 1637-41, by James Gordon and included in the account of Old and Rare Tartans, by Donald Wm. Stewart.

Tours in Scotland, 1677-81, by Thos. Kirk and Ralph
Thoresby. Edited by P. Hume Brown. Edinburgh, David Douglas, 1892.

What is My Tartan, by Frank Adam, F.S.A. Scot.
W. & A. K. Johnston, Edinburgh and London, 1896.

Highland Dress, Arms and Ornaments, by Lord
Archibald Campbell. Archibald Constable & Co.,
2 Whitehall Gardens, 1899.

The Scottish Gael, by James Logan, F.S.A.S. Inverness and Edinburgh. Maclachlan & Stewart,
South Bridge.

Scottish Clans and Their Tartans, W. & A. K. Johnston, Edinburgh and London.

Account of the Northern Invasion in 1630 from
"Memoirs of a Cavalier," by Daniel Defoe, born
1661, son of a butcher, James Foe, parish of
St Gile's, Cripplegate. Seeley Jackson and Halli-
day, 54 Fleet Street, London, 1849.

Description of the West Isles of Scotland, by M.
Martin. London, printed for Andrew Bell at the
Cross Keys and Bible in Cornhill, near Stocks
Market, 1703.

The Past in the Present: What is Civilisation? By
Arthur Mitchell, M.D., LL.D. Edinburgh, David
Douglas, 1880. All rights reserved.

History of the Western Highlands and Isles of Scotland, by Donald Gregory. Wm. Tait, Edinburgh,
1886.

Observations relative to Picturesque Beauty, made in
the year 1776, on several parts of Great Britain,
particularly the Highlands of Scotland, by Wm.
Gilpin, A.M., Prebendary of Salisbury, etc. London, printed for R. Blamire, Strand, 1789.

The Costume of the Clans, by John S. S. Stuart and
Ch. Ed. Stuart. Edinburgh, John Grant, 1892.

A Tour in Scotland and a Voyage to the Hebrides,
1772, by Thos. Pennant. Chester, printed for John
Monk, 1774.

History of the Highlanders and Gaelic Scotland, by
Dugald Mitchell, M.D., Paisley. Alexander Gardner, 1900.

The Antiquary's Book, by Geo. Cinch. Methuen & Co., 36 Essex Street, W.C.

On the Antiquity of the Highland Dress, by Professor Sayce. The Celtic Magazine, 1886-7.

Notes on the Highland Dress and Arms. The Celtic Magazine, vol. vii., 1882.

Sketches of Early Scotch History, by C. Innes (Home Life). Edinburgh, Edmonston and Douglas, 1861.

Letters from a Gentleman in the North of Scotland to his Friend in London. An account of the Highlands, with the Customs and Manners of the Highlanders. (The author is commonly understood to have been Captain Burt, an officer of Engineers, who about 1730 was sent into Scotland as a Contractor). Notes by the Editor, R. Jamieson, F.S.A., Lond. and Edin., Correspondent Member of the Scandinavian Literary Society of Copenhagen. Printed for Rest Fenner, Paternoster Row, 1818.

The Historical Character of the Wars of Torlough, by John, son of Rory MacGrath. Read by Thomas J. Westropp, M.A., Dec. 8th, 1902. Transactions of the Royal Irish Academy, 1902.

Clans and Septs and Regiments of the Scottish Highlands, by Frank Adam. London and Edinburgh, 1908.

Lectures on the Mountains, or the Highlands and the Highlanders. London, Saunders Ottley & Co., 50 Conduit Street, Hanover Square, 1860. (No Author).

Dresses and Decorations of the Middle Ages, by Henry Shaw, F.S.A. London, Wm. Pickering, 1843.

A Collection of Voyages and Travels. London, printed and sold by Thos. Osborne of Gray's Inn, 1745.

The Costumes of the Original Inhabitants of British Islands from the earliest periods to the 6th century, by E. R. Meyrick and C. H. Smith. London, Howlett and Brimmer, 10 Frith Street, Soho Square, 1821.

Notes on Civil Costume in England from the Conquest to the Regency, by the Hon. Lewis Wingfield. London, E. Menken, 41 Gray's Inn Road, 1884.

A Complete History of the Rebellion, by James Ray of Whitehaven, Volunteer under H.R. Duke of Cumberland. Bristol, S. Farley & Co., 1752.

Notes on the Antiquity of Tartan, by Captain Macra Chisholm. The Celtic Magazine, conducted by Alex. Mackenzie, F.S.A. Scot. (Vol. VII.) Inverness, 1882.

The History of British Costume by J. R. Planche, 1874. London, Geo. Bell & Sons, York Street, Covent Garden.

The Book of Costume or Annals of Fashion, by a lady of rank. London, Hy. Colburne, 13 Great Marlborough Street, 1846.

Notes from the Royal Society of Antiquaries of Ireland, 1896, 1900 and 1904. Dublin, University Press.

Observations on a short tour made in the summer of 1803 to the Western Highlands of Scotland. London, 1804. W. Nicholson, Warner Street.

Notes from the History of Manchester on Early Dress, Wool, Linen and Food of the Ancient Britons, by John Whitaker, B.D., F.S.A, 1781. Sold by Messrs Dodsley in Pall Mall.

Encyclopædia of Costume, by J. R. Planche, London, Chatto and Windus, Piccadilly, 1876.

Old and Rare Scottish Tartans, by D. W. Stewart.

The Present State of Scotland. London, 1738.

Leslie's Hist. of Scotland, translated from the Latin to Scotch, by Father James Dalrymple, 1596. Blackwood & Sons, Edinburgh and London, 1886.

Historical Notes on the Highland Dress, by Donald Wm. Stewart, F.S.A. Scot. Edinburgh, printed privately, 1893.

The People of the World, by Dr Robert Brown, M.A. Cassell & Co., Ltd., 1886.

Sketches of the Character, Manners and Present State of the Highlanders of Scotland. Col. David Stewart, Edinburgh, printed for Archibald Constable & Co., 1822.

A Voyage to St. Kilda, the remotest part of all the Hebrides or Western Isles of Scotland, by M. Martin. London, printed for R. Griffith at the Dunciad, in Ludgate, 1749.

The Children of the Mist, by Lord Archibald Campbell. W. & A. K. Johnston, Edinburgh and London, 1890.

Celtic Dyes. The Celtic Magazine, 1883.

Highlands and Western Isles of Scotland, descriptive of their scenery and antiquities, founded on a series of annual journeys between the years 1811 and 1821, and forming a universal guide to that country in letters to Sir Walter Scott, Bart., by John Macculloch, M.D., F.R.S., G.S.L.S. London, Longman, Hurst, Rees, Orme, Brown & Green, Paternoster Row, 1824.

Highland Fabrications and Dress, by John M. Macpherson, Stornoway. The Celtic Magazine, 1884-5.

Journey through Scotland, by the Author of the Journey through England. London, printed for J. Pemberton at the Buck and Son and J. Hooke, at the Flower-de-luce, both against St. Dunstan's Church in Fleet Street, 1729.

Traditions of Edinburgh. Edinburgh, W. Rutherford, 45 Princes Street, 1848.

History of the Highlanders and of the Highland Clans, by James Browne, LL.D. London, Edinburgh and Dublin. A. Fullarton & Co., 1849.

Records of Argyll, by Lord Archibald Campbell. William Blackwood & Sons, Edinburgh and London, 1885.

Mediæval Scotland, by R. W. Cochran-Patrick, LL.D. Glas., LL.B., Cantab, B.A., Edin. Glasgow, James Maclehose & Sons, 1892.

Chamber's Encyclopædia.

Notes and Queries, Note by W. W. Malta, Dec., 1857.

The Grameid, a historical poem descriptive of the Campaign of Viscount Dundee in 1689, by James Philip of Almerieclose 1691. Translated by the Rev. Alex. D. Murdoch, F.S.A.S. for the Scottish History Socy., 1888.

Ancient Scotch Weapons, by James Drummond, R.S.A. Introduction and Descriptive Notes by Joseph Anderson. Edinburgh and London, 1881. George Watson & Sons.

A Short History of the Scotch Highlanders, by W. C. Mackenzie, Paisley, Alex. Gardner, 1908.

Scot's Magazine, 1751. Edinburgh, printed by W. Sands, A. Murray and J. Cochran.

After the Rebellion, by Henry Grey Graham. Glasgow, Jas. Maclehose & Sons, 1902.

Evolution of Clothing by A. E. Garrett and H. F. Tomalin. Adam Bros. and Shardlow, Ltd., 50 Moor Lane, E.C.

Boots and Shoes as exhibited by the worshipful company of Cordwainers, by W. H Dutton, Warden of the Company. London, Chapman and Hall, 11 Henrietta Street, Covent Garden, 1898.

The Evolution of Fashion, by Florence M. Gardiner, London, 1897. The Cotton Press, Granville House, Arundel Street.

Ancient Costume of Great Britain and Ireland from the 7th to the 16th century, by Ch. Hamilton Smith. London, Wm. Bulmer & Co., Shakespeare Press, 1814.

The Heritage of Dress, by Wilfred M. Webb, F. Linnian, S. London. London, The Times Book Club, 1912.

History of Feminine Costume, published by Liberty & Co., Ltd.

Chats on Costume, by G. W. Rhead, R.E. London, T. Fisher Unwin, Adelphi Terrace, 1906.

The Clan of Donald, by Rev. A. Macdonald and Rev. A. Macdonald, Inverness. The Northern Counties Publishing Co., Ltd., 1900.

Tales of a Grandfather (Chapter 39), by Sir Walter Scott. The substance of this narrative was first published in Mr Robert Jameson's introduction to his reprint of Burt's letters from the North of Scotland. From an authentic account of the family of Invernahyle: An MS. communicated to Sir Walter Scott, Bart., by the editor.

Ye Gentle Craft, an illustrated history of Foot-Costume by San Scampion. Northampton, Taylor & Son : London, J. R. Smith, Soho Square, 1876.

Home Life of the Highlanders, by W. M. Mackenzie. Printed for the Highland Village Association, Ltd., by Robert Maclehose & Co., Ltd., Glasgow, 1911.

Official Records of the Mutiny in the Black Watch, by H. D. MacWilliam, 1910.

Catalogue of the Scottish Exhibition of Natural History, Art, and Industry, Glasgow, 1911.

Celtic Scot, by Wm. F. Skene, D.C.L., LL.D., 3 vols. David Douglas, 1886.

The Tartans of the Clans and Septs of Scotland. W. & A. K. Johnston, 1906.

Military Antiquities, by Francis Grose, F.A.S., 1801.

Old English Costumes : Victoria and Albert Museum, 1913.

Letter to a Colonel of a Highland Regiment : Scots' Magazine, 1798.

The Highland Dress, by Sir John Sinclair, Scots' Magazine, 1796.

Clann Shinclair—The Sinclairs. Scottish Journal, Vol. I., 1847-48.

Letters of a Pilgrim in Scotland. Scottish Journal, Vol. I., 1847-48. Edinburgh, T. G. Stevenson.

The Celtic Trews, by David MacRitchie. The Scottish Historical Review, 1904, J. Maclehose & Son, Glasgow.

Journal of a Tour through the Highlands of Scotland during the Summer of 1829, by B. Botfield. Norton Hall, 1830.

Characteristic Dress of the Ancient Scots Highlanders, by the late John Dalrymple. Scots' Magazine, 1796.

The Highlanders of Scotland, by W. F. Skene, D.C.L., LL.D., F.S.A. Scot. Eneas Mackay, 43 Murray Place, Stirling, 1902.

Concise Historical Proofs respecting the Gail of Alban, or Highlanders of Scotland, by James A. Robertson, F.S.A. Scot. Edinburgh, Wm. P. Nimmo, 1867.

The Discovery of a Leather Cloak, by Robert Macadam. Ulster Journal of Archæology, 1861.

Remarks on Local Scenery and Manners in Scotland, by John Stoddart, LL.B. Wm. Millar, Old Bond Street, 1801.

Statistical Account of Scotland, 1791. (See article on Kilwinning).

The Beauties of Scotland, by Robert Forsyth. Edinburgh. John Brown, 1805.

INDEX.

Ancient Britons	... ...	9
Ancient form of Kilt	... ...	15
Ancient Irish	... ...	8
Argyle and Sutherland Highlanders	... ...	26
Armorial Bearings	... ...	17
Aryan Style of Costume	... ...	10
Balmoral Bonnet	... ...	37
Battle of Culloden	... ...	29
Battle of Falkirk	... ...	28
Belt	... ...	22
Belted Plaid	 14,	18
Bibliography	... ...	38
Black Watch	... ...	25
Bonnet	... ... 22, 34,	37
Breacan	... ...	16
Breacan-feile	... ...	14
British Celts	... ...	9
Broad Belt	... ...	35
Broad Sword	 18,	22
Brooch	... ... 14, 35,	37
Brogues	... ... 9, 22,	37
Buckles	 23,	37
Bullet Mould	... ...	22
Buttons	... ...	37
Burt, Captain	 13,	16
Buskins	... ...	9
Cameron Highlanders	... ...	26
Cap	... .	34
Carrying of Arms proscribed	... ...	24
Celtic Race	... .	8
Celts	... ...	16
Chief's Dress	... ...	22
Clan System	... ...	11
Clan System Ended	... ...	29
Claw Brooch	... .	35
Claymore	... ... 18, 35,	37
Coatee	... ...	33
Collar and Tie	... ...	36
Colours	 9,	12
Condition of Scotland	... ...	13
Cope, Sir John	... ...	28
Crest	... ...	37
Culloden	... ...	28
Cumberland, Duke of	... ...	28
Darloch	... ...	20
Dirk	... ...18, 22, 34,	37
Disarming the Highlanders	... ...	25
Doublet	... ... 22, 32,	37
Dwellings	... ...	13
Eighteenth Century Costume	... .	23

INDEX—contd.

Falkirk, Battle of	...	...	...	...	...	28
Feudalism	...	...	...	...	...	10
Feile Beg	...	...	...	...	...	18
Fillibeg	...	...	...	...	... 18,	21
Flanders	...	...	...	...	...	25
Fontenoy	...	..	...	...	...	25
Foot Wear	...	...	...	...	...	34
Fork ...	...	...	...	19, 22,	35,	37
Gaiters	...	...	..	...	... 22,	36
Garters	...	...	...	...	...	23
Gauls ...	...	...	...	...	...	9
George I.	...	...	...	...	...	20
Glenfinnan	...	...	...	...	...	27
Glengarry Bonnet	...	...	...	...	...	37
Gordon Highlanders		...	...	...	...	26
Gordons	...	...	...	...	...	11
Goths ...	...	...	...	...	...	16
Habits of Highlanders in Battle		...	...	...	...	19
Highland Chief's Dress		...	...	...	...	22
Highland Clan System		...	...	...	...	10
Highland Companies		...	...	...	...	25
Highland Light Infantry		...	...	...	...	26
Highland Looms	...	...	...	...	...	15
Highland Plaid	...	...	...	...	...	14
Highland Regiments		...	...	...	...	26
Hints on Scottish National Dress		...	...	...	...	32
Hose ...	..	...	...	...	...	22
Jabot ...	...	...	...	...	... 35,	37
Jacobites	...	...	...	...	...	27
Kilt	...	...	...	...	...10, 21, 32,	37
Kilted Plaid	..	...	...	...	...	14
Kilt Pin	...	...	...	...	..	37
Knife ...	...	...	...	...	...19, 22, 35,	37
Ladies' Dress	...	...	...	...	...	36
Ladies of Edinburgh		...	...	...	...	30
Little Kilt	...	...	...	...	...	18
Lowlanders	...	...	...	...	...	16
Malcolm Canmore ...		...	...	...	...	10
M'Intyre North's Views		...	...	...	...	18
"Mercurious Scotticus"		...	...	...	...	17
Moore's Retreat to Corunna		...	...	...	..	23
Morning Dress	...	...	...	...	...	36
Mutiny of the Black Watch		...	...	...	...	26
Norman-French Refugées ...		...	...	...	...	10
Ornaments...	...	...	...	..	 34,	37
Peninsular War	...	...	...	...	...	23
Pinkerton's Views	...	...	...	...	...	17
Pistols...	...	...	...	...	... 18,	22
Plaid ...	...	...	...	...	... 22, 33,	37
Powder Horn	...	...	...	...	... 19,	35
Pre-historic Times	...	...	...	...	...	7

INDEX—contd.

Primitive Scotland	10
Prince Charlie's Military Movements	27
Prohibition of use of Ancient Clothing	19
Purse 19, 22
Queen's Own Cameron Highlanders	26
Raising the Stuart Standard	27
Ramsay, Allan	21
Rebellion of 1715	20
Retreat of Highlanders	28
Roman Invasion	10
Sashes	36
Saxon Refugees	10
Sclavonic Tribes	16
Scottish Dress	7
Scottish National Dress	7
Sculptured Stones	17
Seaforth Highlanders	26
Sheath Knife	35
Shoe Buckles... ... ... 23, 37
Shoulder Belt	37
Shoulder Brooch	37
Side Pouch	20
Silver Buckles	35
Silver Buttons	24
Silver Chains	24
Silver Chain Strap	37
Skean-dhu 23, 35, 37
Soaking the Plaid	15
Sporran 15, 19, 23, 35, 37
Stockings 22, 34, 37
Stuart, Prince Charles Edward	27
Stuart, Prince James	20
Suppression of Highland Dress	20
Sutherland Highlanders	26
Target	19
Target with Spear	22
Tartan	16
"Tartana, or The Plaid"	21
Tartan Dresses	10
Tartan in The Lowlands	30
Tartan Prohibited	29
Tartan Sashes	36
Tie	33
Trews... ... ... 34, 37
Vest	32
Wade, General	25
Waist Belt	37
Weapons	18
Wearing of The Kilt Proscribed	24
Weaving	12
Wetting The Plaid	15

Printed by David Davidson, St John's Printing Works, Leith.